TRACTORS

by Amanda Doering Tourville
illustrated by Zachary Trover

Content Consultant:
Paul M. Goodrum, PE, PhD, Associate Professor
Department of Civil Engineering, University of Kentucky

visit us at www.abdopublishing.com

Published by Magic Wagon, a division of the ABDO Group, 8000 West 78th Street, Edina, Minnesota, 55439. Copyright © 2009 by Abdo Consulting Group, Inc. International copyrights reserved in all countries. All rights reserved. No part of this book may be reproduced in any form without written permission from the publisher.

Looking Glass Library™ is a trademark and logo of Magic Wagon.

Printed in the United States.

Text by Amanda Doering Tourville
Illustrations by Zachary Trover
Edited by Patricia Stockland
Cover and interior design by Emily Love

Library of Congress Cataloging-in-Publication Data
Tourville, Amanda Doering, 1980-
  Tractors / by Amanda Doering Tourville ; illustrated by Zachary Trover.
     p. cm. — (Mighty machines)
  Includes index.
  ISBN 978-1-60270-626-2
  1. Tractors—Juvenile literature. I. Trover, Zachary, ill. II. Title.
  TL233.15.T58 2009
  629.225'2—dc22
                2008036004

Table of Contents

What Is a Tractor?

A tractor is a machine that pulls farm equipment in the fields. Tractors can also push dirt, snow, and other materials. Some small tractors are used for lawn and garden work. Tractors come in different shapes and sizes depending on the work that they do.

Types of Tractors

There are two types of tractors. There are wheeled tractors and crawler tractors. Wheeled tractors sit on large, rubber tires. These tires are grooved so that they can grip the ground underneath them. Wheeled tractors can have three or four wheels.

Some large wheeled tractors have double tires on each wheel. The extra wheels give the tractor more traction. The rear tires of a tractor are usually larger than the front tires.

Crawler tractors move on tracks instead of tires. These tracks are wide metal belts that move forward or backward. Tracks allow the tractor to move without sinking into soft dirt or mud.

Crawler tractors are often used in very hilly areas. They don't tip over as easily as wheeled tractors might.

Parts of Tractors

The driver operates the tractor from the cab. Some small tractors don't have a cab. Instead, they just have a driver's seat.

Wheeled tractors have a steering wheel like large trucks. Crawler tractors have levers or joysticks to control the tracks. Tractors also have foot pedals that make the machine move and stop.

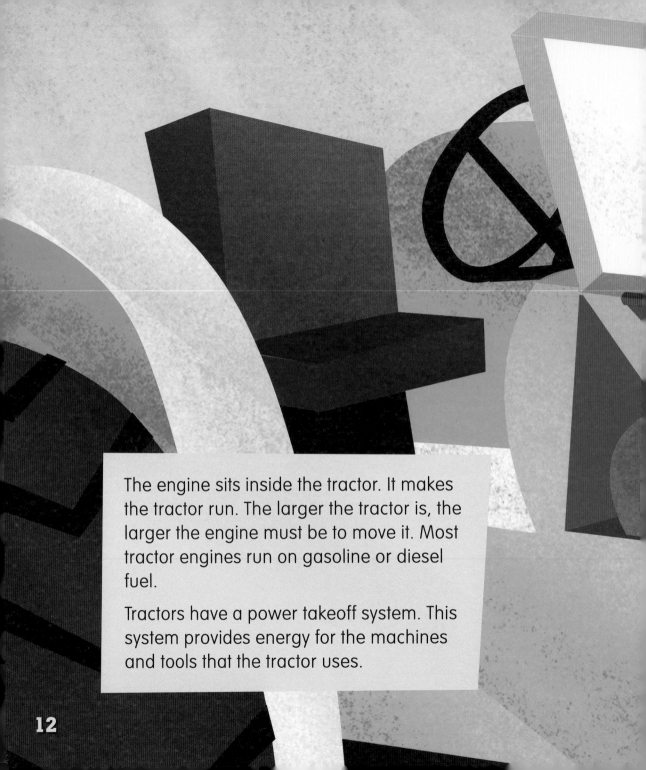

The engine sits inside the tractor. It makes the tractor run. The larger the tractor is, the larger the engine must be to move it. Most tractor engines run on gasoline or diesel fuel.

Tractors have a power takeoff system. This system provides energy for the machines and tools that the tractor uses.

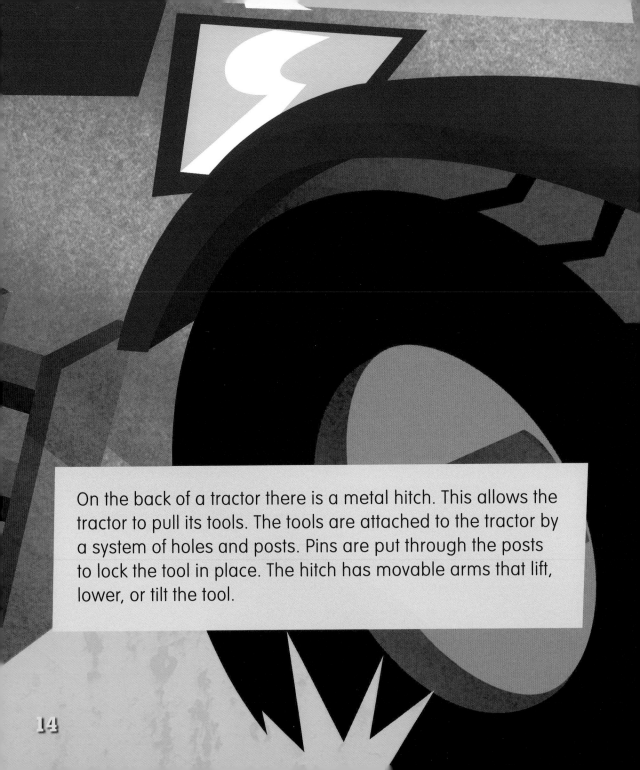

On the back of a tractor there is a metal hitch. This allows the tractor to pull its tools. The tools are attached to the tractor by a system of holes and posts. Pins are put through the posts to lock the tool in place. The hitch has movable arms that lift, lower, or tilt the tool.

Tools for Tractors

There are machines and tools that are pulled behind tractors. On the farm, these tools are used to work the soil and plant and harvest crops. A plow digs into the land and turns it over. A seed drill plants seeds. A baler picks up hay and shapes it into bales. And, a brush hog cuts grass and brush.

Some tractors push the tools. Snowplows and bulldozer blades can be attached to the front of these tractors. The tractors plow snow in the winter. They also move earth in the spring, summer, and fall.

How Are Tractors Used?

Tractors are mostly used for farming land. Tractors and farm tools loosen soil, plant seeds, and harvest crops.

Small tractors can mow yards and plow and plant gardens. They also move rock and earth for landscaping.

21

Tractors are also used to construct buildings and roads. Some tractors use bulldozer blades to push dirt and gravel. Other tractors pull scrapers that level the land.

Where Are Tractors Used?

Tractors are used all over the world. Tractors work at construction sites and help plow snow. Small tractors in suburban areas help people mow their yards.

Tractors are mostly used on farms in the country.
They help farmers grow food.

Tractors Are Mighty Machines!

Tractors are built strong to do important jobs. They help grow the food we eat. Tractors help construct our buildings and roads. And, they move snow so we can get around in the winter. Tractors are mighty machines!

Tractor Parts

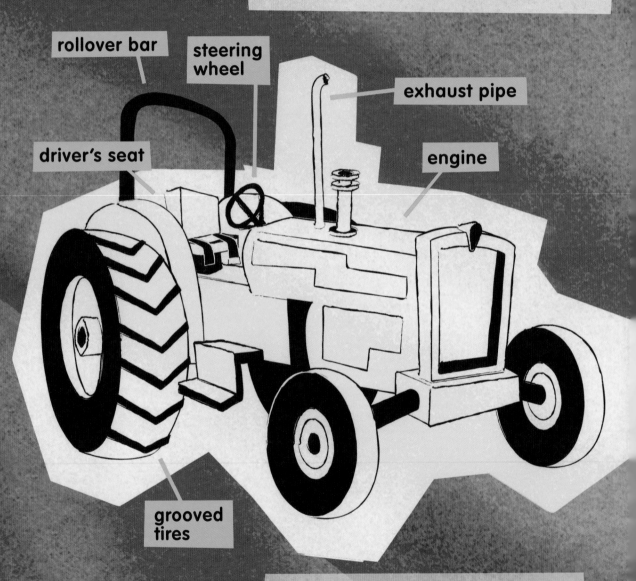

rollover bar

steering wheel

exhaust pipe

driver's seat

engine

grooved tires

Cabless Wheeled Tractor

headlights

cab

exhaust pipe

hitch

blade tool

engine

metal track

Crawler Tractor

29

Fun Facts

⚙ Tractors used to have metal wheels. The wheels had metal plates or spikes that stuck out of the wheel. These plates or spikes gave the wheels traction.

⚙ Before tractors, farmers used teams of horses to pull the farm tools. Now, large tractor engines have the power of 200 horses!

⚙ Steam-engine tractors were first made in the late 1800s. At first, many people thought they were silly. These people did not believe that machines would ever replace horses and manpower.

⚙ Many tractors have strong headlights so that they can work in the dark.

⚙ The tires of a giant tractor can be taller than a human.

⚙ A giant tractor can have as many as 12 tires. These tires spread out the weight of the huge tractor body.

Glossary

construction—the act of building or making something.

equipment—the tools or resources that help a person do something.

harvest—to gather a crop.

landscaping—the act of changing the appearance of the land in a decorative way, usually with plants.

suburban—relating to a smaller community outside a city.

tilt—to move into a slanted position.

traction— friction between a body and the surface on which it moves, enabling the body to move without slipping.

Web Sites

To learn more about tractors, visit ABDO Group online at **www.abdopublishing.com**. Web sites about tractors are featured on our Book Links page. These links are routinely monitored and updated to provide the most current information available.

Index